KV-635-910

Lucille Ball

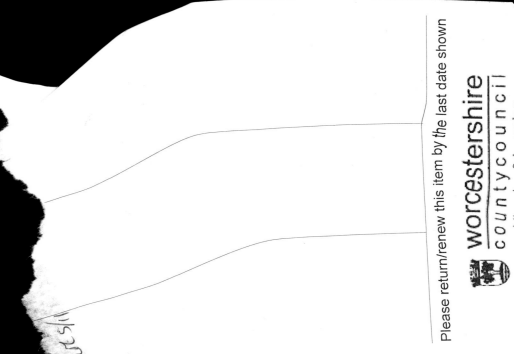

Please return/renew this item by the last date shown

worcestershire
countycouncil
Libraries & Learning

700037464322

Lucille Ball

Nick Yapp

endeavour

Copyright © Endeavour London 2010

Lucille Ball is part of the series of books on Hollywood and Rock Icons. The design was initiated by Paul Welti, but created by Ros Holder. Author Nick Yapp worked closely with picture researcher Jennifer Jeffrey. The book was edited by Mark Fletcher and proofread by Liz Ihre. Mary Osborne led the production.

All rights reserved. No part of this publication may be reproduced, stored in a retrieval system, or transmitted, in any form or by any means, electronic, mechanical, photocopying, recording, or otherwise, without prior written permission from the publisher.

Endeavour London Ltd
21-31 Woodfield Road
London W9 2BA

ISBN 978-1-873913-32-1

Printed and bound in Singapore
1 3 5 7 9 10 8 6 4 2

Frontispiece: One of the many faces of Lucille from a photo shoot in the early 1940s.
Title Page: A scene from *I Love Lucy*, Episode 23— *The Moustache*, which was aired on March 17, 1952.

Above: The Lucille Ball Stamp from August 2001. She was the seventh actor to be honored on a commemorative postage stamp in the Legends of Hollywood Series.

Contents

Introduction

Lucille Désirée Ball was born in her grandparents' apartment in Jamestown, New York State, at five in the afternoon on August 6, 1911. Her father was Henry Durrell Ball, a Baptist of Scottish descent who worked as a linesman for the Michigan Bell Company. Her mother was Désirée "DeDe" Evelyn Ball (née Hunt), whose ancestors were a mixture of French, English, and Irish. Lucille (*above, in her christening robe*) was their first child, to be followed four years later by her brother Fred. The family moved from Jamestown to Anaconda, Montana, and then to Wyancotte, Michigan.

In 1915, when DeDe was expecting their second child, Henry contracted typhoid and died. Lucille was then a three-year-old (*right*), and the trauma of that time remained with her throughout her life. "I do remember everything that happened," she later recalled. "Hanging out of the window, begging to play with the kids next door, who had measles; the doctor coming, my mother weeping… a bird that flew in the window, a picture that fell off the wall…" Not long after the death of Henry, DeDe remarried. Lucille was passed from one set of grandparents to another, the worst of whom was Sophia Peterson, DeDe's new mother-in-law. Sophia could have sprung straight from *Grimm's Fairy Tales*. She mocked Lucille for her feet (too large), her teeth (too crooked), and her voice (too loud). Mercifully, Lucille finally ending up back in Jamestown with her mother's parents, while DeDe and her new husband decamped to search for work.

It was Grandfather Hunt, a socialist and a lover of the theater, who introduced Lucille to showbiz. He took her to vaudeville shows at Shea's and The Palace, where she fell in love with the whole idea of making people laugh, and to the silent movies where comedy was then entirely visual.

Chapter 1

The Queen of the Bs

1933–1949

Previous page: Venus Arising…
a promotional portrait for *Roman
Scandals*, made in 1933. Lucille is
dressed in the flesh-colored body-
stocking in which she and her
fellow slave girls emerged from the
Baths. The costume design was the
idea of Busby Berkeley.

Right: Variety celebrates the birth
of the Dionne Quins, November
1935. (*left to right, in baby carriages*)
Maxine Jennings, Virginia Carrege,
Lucille, Margaret Nacarge, and Joy
Nodges. Tony Martin plays the part
of the Doctor (*far right*).

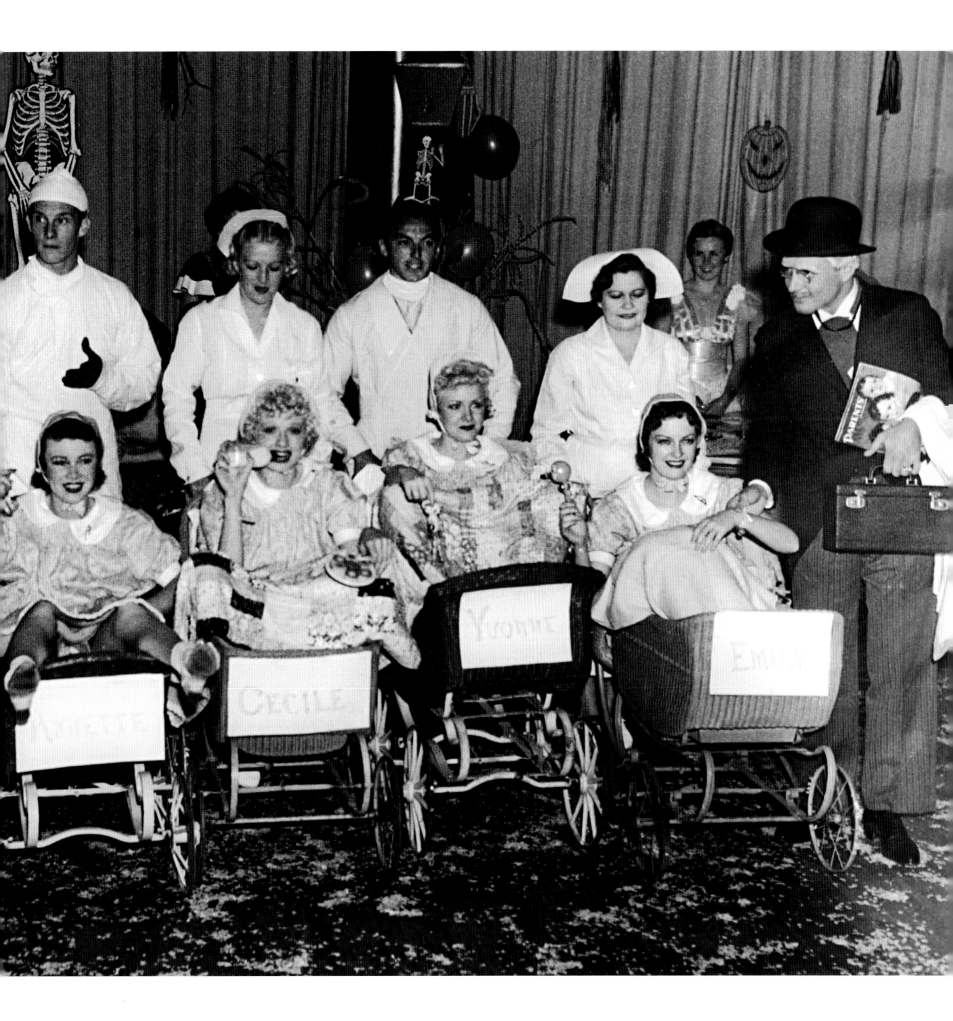

Above: Lucille with Hollywood actor Jon Hall (*standing behind*) and actor/director Alexander Hall (*seated*) at the Trocadero, Los Angeles, 1934. By that time, Lucille had already played small parts in four films.

Opposite: Doing the rounds on the Hollywood scene... Lucille on a date with Alexander Hall, a man who was seventeen years older than she was. "She was a peach, he was a beast," said a friend.

Years of Setback

If Grandfather Hunt planted the showbiz seed, it was DeDe who transplanted the seedling. She had little choice. Lucille, at the age of fourteen, had started dating Jamestown's local "badboy" Johnny DeVita—dark, smart, dangerous, and possessor of a car. So DeDe packed her daughter off to New York City, where Lucille enrolled in the Robert Minton–John Murray Anderson School for the Dramatic Arts.

She arrived with $50 sewn into her underwear and high hopes, which were quickly dashed. "I was a tongue-tied teenager, spellbound by the school's star pupil, Bette Davis," said Lucille. "All I learned at drama school was how to be frightened." The School's drama coaches thought little of her acting, claiming she had "no future at all as a performer". She returned home, deeply disillusioned.

Two years later she was back in New York, to suffer another setback when she became crippled with what was probably rheumatic fever, and for two years was unable to do any work. In 1932, it was a matter of third time lucky. She was offered a job as a model by fashion designer Hattie Carnegie. With a figure that was considered too slim for most modelling work at that time, Lucille specialized in hats and heavy fur coats and wraps. Hattie was a kind employer, and it was through her that Lucille had her first break when she was selected as The Chesterfield Girl.

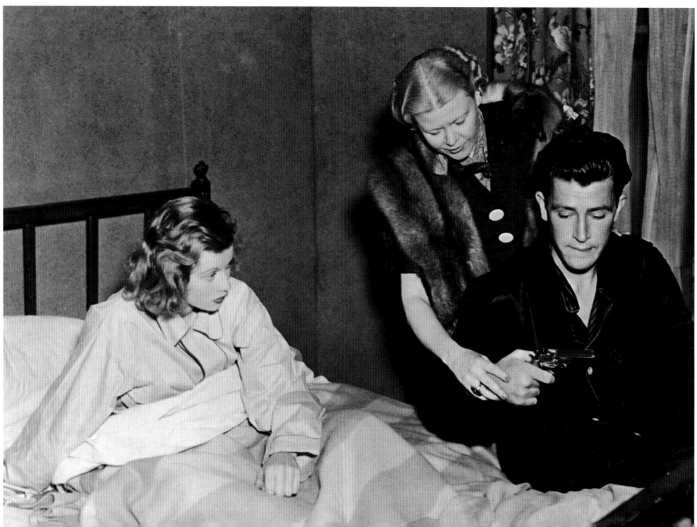

Early Days in Hollywood

Lucille's career as a performer began inauspiciously on Broadway in 1932. Under her stage name of Diane Belmont (named after the racetrack), she was hired for and fired from both Earl Carroll's *Vanities* and Flo Ziegfeld's third touring company of *Rio Rita*, and was then "let go" by the Shubert Brothers from their production of *Stepping Stones*. She was lucky to meet Sam Goldwyn's assistant Jim Mulvey, who chose her as the thirteenth Goldwyn Girl (there were supposed to be only twelve) and shipped her out to Hollywood.

In her early movies, Lucille was invariably cast as some sort of dancer: a "chorine" in *Murder at the Vanities*, a dancing slave girl in *Roman Scandals*, a "dance girl" in *Kid Millions*, and a chorus girl in *Bottoms Up*. In 1934, she appeared in a Three Stooges short entitled *Three Little Pigskins*, in which she was supposed to be on the receiving end of a seltzer squirt. "The best thing I learned from the Stooges," Lucille said later, "was when to duck." Her natural talent for visual comedy passed unnoticed by studio boss Harry Cohn, who "didn't think she had any talent" and fired her.

She kept going, determined to succeed. She found regular work was just that, although the pay was not great—around $50 a week.

Opposite above: Lela Rogers (*left*) coaches a group of aspiring young Hollywood actresses, including Lucille Ball (*center*).

Opposite below: Lucille, in bed, watches as Lela Rogers helps another Hollywood wannabe, John Shelton, 1936.

Above: Lucille applies make-up to the eyebrows of American boxer and former Light Heavyweight Champion of the World "Slapsie Maxie" Rosenbloom on the set of Charles Vidor's film *Muss 'em Up*, 1936.

Above: Actor Frank Albertson looks on while the finishing touches are added to Lucille's hair style before shooting a scene for William A. Seiter's Marx Brothers comedy *Room Service,* 1938.

Opposite: Lucille did not enjoy making *Room Service,* a film produced by Pandro S. Berman, with whom she was having an affair. She liked Harpo Marx, but her dislike of Groucho was mutual. "I've never found Lucille Ball to be funny on her own," said Groucho years later, "she's always needed a script".

"If an actress has the slightest aversion to pie in the face,
the camera will pick it up instantly" – Lucille

Left: Lucille on tour in an automobile-trailer that was "the exact duplicate" of the one featured in RKO's *Go Chase Yourself,* 1938.
Opposite: Still in her blonde days, Lucille models a fur in the early 1940s. She enjoyed and needed modelling work, and Hollywood studios executives were impressed by the fact that she had modelled for Bergdorf Goodman in New York.

A New Queen is Crowned

The titles of the films in which Lucille was handed a part under the studio system suggest a mixture of light comedy and featherweight drama. But many of the scripts were well crafted, with witty dialogue that Lucille delivered far better than most. The parts were still those of stock characters: a blonde telephone operator (*Broadway Bill*), a blonde beauty operator (*Fugitive Lady*), a blonde fashion model (*Roberta*), despite the fact that Lucille was a brunette.

Nevertheless, something was happening. Her own enthusiasm, energy, and powers of observation, coupled with endless nights and weekends studying acting, were bringing her to the attention of people that mattered in Hollywood. In 1938 she played the lead role in *The Affairs of Annabel*, a film sufficiently successful to be followed by *Annabel Takes a Holiday* in the same year. Lucille was even one of the many considered for the role of Scarlett O'Hara in *Gone with the Wind*, but her audition with David O. Selznick was a farce. Caught in a rain shower, Lucille arrived dripping wet. Fortified with a brandy, she had to audition on her knees. She failed to get the part.

In Lucille's early Hollywood days, Fay Wray had held the title of "Queen of the Bs"—the support films that were an essential part of a double-bill program in the economically tough 1930s. Lucille had played supporting roles in a few of Wray's movies and, after Wray's retirement from movies in 1942, the title was passed on to Lucille. There was no crown to go with the title; had there been, it would have been placed, not on the head of a brunette or a blonde, but of a flaming redhead. In 1943, Lucy was introduced on the radio show *Daffy's Tavern* as "the termater (tomato) with the carrot hair… very nutritious".

Left: Phil Baker and Lucille at the mike during a transmission of *The Phil Baker Show* in 1938. Like Lucille, Baker was a popular guest on such radio shows as *The Jack Benny Show, Duffy's Tavern,* and *The Burns and Allen Show.*

"Don't pay any attention to her... she's great at parties, a real funny kid, but I can't see any future for her in movies" - Pandro S. Berman on Lucille

Radio Ham

Lucille's first break into the popular and profitable world of radio came in 1937, when she was invited to appear as a regular on the CBS *Gulf Headliner* series. The show was fronted by Phil Baker, an ex-vaudeville star, and an experienced, though nervous, performer. Lucille stayed on the show from 1937 to 1938, and then joined *The Wonder Show*, sponsored by Wonder Bread and hosted by Jack Haley, later to be the Tin Man in *The Wizard of Oz.*

It was here that Lucille found her radio feet. "Radio work," she recalled, "gave me a name in the trade as a good female foil. I could flip a comedy line, which a lot of actresses couldn't do... I had to rely on timing and tone of voice for comic effects, and this was invaluable training..." It was also on *The Wonder Show* that Lucille began a professional relationship with announcer Gale Gordon that was to last for fifty years.

Above: A production still from the 1941 RKO film *Look Who's Laughing:* (*left to right*) Marian Jordan, Lucille, Jim Jordan, and the ventriloquist Edgar Bergen. Marian and Jim Jordan were the stars of radio's *Fibber McGee and Molly.*

Opposite: Mixing with other "bad boys"… (*left to right*) Virginia Pine, George Raft, Mack "Killer" Gray, and Lucille share a box at a racetrack in the early 1940s. Lucille dated Gray for a while; his "Killer" nickname was given to him because he had undergone surgery for a hernia, and the Yiddish for hernia is *killa.*

" It's very difficult to get a satisfactory picture of Miss Ball because the lady
is just not photogenic" - T. Henry Black, Jamestown's local photographer

Opposite far left: An untypically glamorous portrait of Lucille taken by photographer Walters Sanders in December 1942.

Opposite left: Lucille dances across the screen in the 1942 RKO film *The Big Street*, in which Lucille starred with Henry Fonda. It was Lucille's favorite among all her films.

Above: Another 1942 Sanders portrait of Lucille in her dressing room.

Opposite: Lucille appears in an ad promoting Shaefer Beer, 1944. At the time, Shaefer was the world's best selling beer.
Left: Lucille reads through a radio script with Bing Crosby in 1944, when Crosby was to be heard on both *The Kraft Music Hall* and American Forces Radio.
Below: MGM stars gather to celebrate President Roosevelt's birthday, January 29, 1944. (*left to right, front row*) Brian Aherne, Jeanne Cagney (sister of Jimmy), Commissioner Russ Young, Lucille, and Walter Pidgeon.

A Change of Studio

In 1943, Lucille left RKO and signed with the more prestigious Metro-Goldwyn-Mayer, whose glorious use of Technicolor could do justice to her new hair color. She was now a confirmed redhead—"Once in his life," she joked, "every man has to fall in love with a gorgeous redhead" and, in the darkness of the movie palaces of the 1940s, just about every man did.

Perhaps the two aspects of life at MGM that Lucille most appreciated was the irony of appearing in the film version of *The Ziegfeld Follies*, and the joy of sharing an office with Buster Keaton. Lucille greatly admired Keaton and in the *I Love Lucy* years she paid tribute to him: "He taught me most of what I know about timing, how to fall, and how to handle pros and animals".

Opposite: Lucille in fashion mode, August 13, 1945—cool and elegant, but the days when she could seriously project this image of herself in public were numbered.

Left: Lucille at the keyboard with her mother, DeDe Ball. The picture was taken at Lucille's farm in Chatsworth, California, at the time when she was making *Easy to Wed* for MGM. DeDe Ball was a pianist of concert standard.

A Class Act

Lucille scored a big hit with her first movies for MGM, most of which were high class, high budget films put together by some of the best talent in Hollywood. In *Dubarry Was a Lady* (1943), based on a Broadway musical with music and lyrics by Cole Porter, Lucille played opposite Red Skelton and a young Gene Kelly. In *Thousands Cheer,* she was one of many guest stars (others included Lena Horne and Judy Garland), a sure sign that she was getting very near the top of the tree. She was, however, still a loyal trooper, prepared to do almost anything demanded of her by her studio—such as appearing in *Abbott and Costello in Hollywood* (1945).

She was also still a glamorous model, although she had reservations about her looks, and was conscious that she was slim by Hollywood standards. "I don't do T and A (known in the business as "tits and ass") very well," she said, "because I don't have much of either."

Above: Orson Welles and Lucille
dine out together in about 1947. By
this time, Lucille was described not as
an "actress", but as a "comedienne".
"I never thought I was funny," she
wrote. "I don't think funny."

Above left: Lucille chats with comedian Ed Wynn at the Annual Circus Benefit for Saint John's Hospital, Los Angeles, July 1, 1948. The event took the form of a real Barnum and Bailey Circus Performance with a cast of Hollywood stars.

Above right: At the same event: (*left to right*) Ed Wynn with his son Keenan Wynn, Lucille, and Desi Arnaz.

" I was very appreciative of the studio system because I had no talent" - Lucille

Above: Desi Arnaz (*center*) interrupts Lucille and Richard Denning during a script reading for a 1949 episode of *My Favorite Husband.*

Opposite: The stage setting for the Saturday evening transmission of *My Favorite Husband.* At the mike are Lucille and Richard Denning, far left is announcer Bob Le Mond, and Musical Director Wilbur Hatch is center, with his back to the camera.

My Favorite Husband

In 1942, Paramount Pictures made *Are Husbands Necessary,* a film starring Ray Milland and Betty Field. The film was based on Isabel Scott Rorick's 1940 novel, *Mr. and Mrs. Cugat,* but it was the radio adaptation of that book that took the public's fancy. The show was called *My Favorite Husband* and ran for 124 episodes, from July 23, 1948 to March 31, 1951, by which time it was hotly tipped to transfer to television.

The radio show, sponsored by General Foods Jell-O, featured Richard Denning and Lucille Ball as Liz and George Cugat, residents of the fictional town of Sheridan Falls. After a few episodes, however, the lead characters'

family name was changed to Cooper, to avoid confusion with the then extremely popular bandleader, Xavier Cugat. The social standing of the main characters was also altered by the show's three writers, Bob Carroll Junior, Madelyn Pugh, and Jess Oppenheimer—all of whom transferred to *I Love Lucy* when the radio series came to an end. The wealthy and socially ambitious Cugats became the middle-class Coopers, and Liz Cooper became increasingly zany, clumsy, and scatter-brained.

It was a happy show. Lucille thoroughly enjoyed working with Denning, and also with her old friend Gale Gordon from *The Phil Baker Show,*

who played the part of Rudolph Atterbury, a friend of George Cooper. She had at last found almost the perfect vehicle for her talents, and strangely it was radio that convinced her she was a visual comic. She noticed that the laughs coming from the studio audience when she pulled faces at the mike, were bigger than the laughs she got from the script. The more she played up to this, the bigger the laughs.

By 1951, CBS were desperate to transfer *My Favorite Husband,* lock, stock and barrel to television, but Lucille had other ideas.

Showbiz—The First Twenty Years

As the 1940s drew to an end, Lucille reached the halfway point in her career. Behind lay struggle, disappointment, and sometimes painfully slow professional progress; ahead lay the great unknown. She had a handful of movies still to make—including two hugely successful films with one of her favorite comedians, Bob Hope—*Sorrowful Jones* in 1949, and *Fancy Pants* in 1950—and there was always radio, or so it seemed at the time.

It was in Lucille's nature to take a largely sanguine view of both her personal and professional life. "One of the things I learned the hard way," she wrote, "was that it doesn't pay to get discouraged. Keeping busy and making optimism a way of life can restore your faith in yourself… I have an everyday religion that works for me. Love yourself first and everything falls into line. You really have to love yourself to get anything done in this world."

The restless teenager who had set off for New York City back in the 1920s, yearning to "make some noise", was now a married woman in her late thirties. She had no money worries, was respected and admired by her colleagues, and was adored by her fans. She longed to have children, but this was proving difficult—she had one miscarriage in 1942, and another in 1949. She considered herself neither lucky nor unlucky in the hand that Fate had dealt her so far, saying: "I don't know anything about luck. I've never banked on it. Luck to me is something else: hard work, and realising what is opportunity and what isn't".

What Lucille did not know in 1949 was that television, destroyer of the studio system that lay at the heart of her movie career, was about to hand her success on a plate.

Above: On location for the 1949 comedy movie *Miss Grant Takes Richmond*, in which Lucille starred with William Holden. It was a happy movie for Lucille, with plenty of scope for her comedic talent: (*left to right*) Lucille, Holden, director Lloyd Bacon, and Frank McHugh, with Jimmie Gleason standing in dark glasses.

"When MGM was grooming you, you felt you were in the second line of the harem" – Lucille

Above: Hollywood stars line up at the train depot *en route* to entertain troops in Ensenada, Mexico during World War II: (*left to right*) Marc Sandrich, Lucille, Jimmy Cagney, Joan Blondell, Stan Laurel, Dick Powell, Jinx Falkenberg, Ann Miller, and Oliver Hardy.

Chapter 2

I Love Desi

1940-1960

Above left: Lucille and Desi in March 1941, a few months after their marriage. At this time, Lucille was described as looking at Desi "as if he were something that had floated down from above on a cloud…"

Center: Lucille and Desi at the Mocambo, Los Angeles, July 1942.

Right: Another club, another cuddle… Desi was drafted into the US Forces in May 1943, just after he became an American citizen.

"Whatta Hunk of a Woman"

In her autobiography—*Love, Lucy*—Lucille describes her first meeting with Desiderio Alberto Arnaz y de Acha III, better known as Desi Arnaz. They met on the lot at RKO, where Lucille was filming *Dance, Girl, Dance*. "I was wearing a slinky gold lamé dress slit up to my thigh, and my long reddish-gold hair fell over my bare shoulders. I also sported a fake black eye, where my lover had supposedly socked me… Desi reared back at the sight of me. 'Whatta hunk of a woman!' he gasped."

Arnaz's recollection of the meeting was a little different. He wasn't smitten until later that day when a refreshed and un-black-eyed, blonde Lucille appeared, dressed in sweater and tight-fitting slacks. Accompanied by other members of the film's cast, they went to lunch at a nearby restaurant and spent the afternoon flirting with each other. "It wasn't love at first sight," wrote Lucille. "It took a full five minutes."

The man that she had fallen for was tall, dark, and handsome, with some similarity to Lucille's first ever *beau*, the dangerous Johnny DeVita. Arnaz was also six years younger than Lucille. He came from a wealthy Cuban family who had fallen on hard times as a result of the Cuban Revolution of 1933. Arnaz and his parents fled to Miami, where he learned English, worked in a pet store, and sang with a Latin-American band. His professional progress was a sprint compared with Lucille's marathon, and by 1938 he was singing with Xavier Cugat's band at the Waldorf-Astoria in New York and appearing on Broadway in George Abbott's musical *Too Many Girls*. When it was decided to turn the show into a movie, Arnaz was invited to Hollywood. A few days later, Desi met Lucille and the wild and bumpy romance began.

The Hollywood Scene in the early
days of Lucille and Desi…
Left above: Lucille and Desi with
bandleader Darryl Harpa, at the
Copacabana, August 1941. Harpa
and his Orchestra had appeared
in the 1939 movie *Rhumba Land*.
Left below: At a charity occasion
organized by Louis B. Mayer.

Above: In the early days of marriage, still starry-eyed, and with what might have been a gift on the table.

"He was the Elvis Presley of his day...
a stunningly good-looking male who was
not only thrilling, but funny" - Lucille on Desi

Left: Another Latin admirer… Cesar Romero whispers a little nothing in the ear of Lucille. Years later, Romero was a featured guest star in the first of the Desi–Lucy one-hour TV Comedy Specials.
Opposite: Lucille and Desi with Maxie Rosenbloom, at "Slapsie Maxie's" nightclub in Los Angeles for the opening of the Dean Martin and Jerry Lewis double act.

Love and Marriage

Desi was at first the courtly knight, who was very protective (which Lucille found irresistible) and who showered his lady fair with gifts and "thousands" of telegrams. He went on tour with his band while she toured to publicize the movie *Too Many Girls*. They missed each other terribly, but both wondered what the other might be up to. To put an end to the misery of separation and the agony of suspicion, they eloped and were married in New York

When they returned to California, they lived at first in Lucille's apartment, where among other friends they entertained Carmen Miranda, Carole Lombard and Clark Gable. A year or so later, they bought a property in Devonshire Drive, surrounded by a white picket fence and five acres of orange trees. Neither had the money to buy it outright, so they took out a ten-year mortgage.

Opposite: A Cuban style and Latin flavor publicity shot… Lucille samples some of Desi's cooking at home in 1944. Many of the ideas for *I Love Lucy* shows came from their real-life marriage.

Left: Desi and Lucille take a bow at the Strand Theater, New York City, June 1950. They were on tour as a double act, shortly after launching Desilu Productions Inc.

"Friends gave our marriage six months; me, I gave it a week" – Lucille

"Complete, Healthy, and Beautiful"

As she had done with her professional life, Lucille threw all her energy into her marriage.

Above all, she longed to have children. She had already suffered two miscarriages and was frightened, as well as elated, when she discovered after ten years of marriage that she was again pregnant. Desi spent $23,000 on adding a nursery wing to their ranch-house home, but it was not to be. Lucille suffered a third miscarriage.

She returned to movies, but gleefully turned down a part in Cecil B. DeMille's *The Greatest Show on Earth* when she discovered that, at the age of forty, she was again pregnant. There followed what Lucille described as "the best year of my marriage to Desi… I was so proud of that big stomach of mine". All went well, and on July 17, 1951 Lucie Désirée arrived. In Lucille's words, "she was complete, healthy, and beautiful".

Eighteen months later, the family was completed by the arrival of Desiderio Alberto Arnaz IV on January 19, 1953.

Opposite, clockwise from top left: Eating for two, Lucille helps herself from the buffet table; at Desi Junior's christening; Lucie examines her baby brother in one of a series of pictures for the cover of *Life* magazine, April 6, 1953; Lucie's first birthday cake, July 17, 1952; Desi and a pregnant Lucille at the Palm Springs Racquet Club a few weeks before the arrival of Desi Junior.

Previous pages: Lucille, Desi, and in two shots little Lucie at home.
Above: A promo for a New Year's Day *I Love Lucy* TV Special, December 16, 1953.

Above: Desi never lost his boyhood love of fishing, and *Desilu* was one of the first fruits of the success of *I Love Lucy*.
Center: A family group in yachting attire: (*left to right*) Lolita Arnaz, Lucille with Lucie, Desi, and Lucille's mother, DeDe.
Right: Desi, Lucille, and Lucie on board the *Desilu*.

"Desi would disappear. It was go, go, go all the time: to the golf links, to his new motel, the gambling tables, or his yacht" - Lucille

Left: Happy days by the poolside… One of the five pet spaniels and Desi and Lucille pose for a magazine picture story of "Hollywood Stars and Their Homes".
Right: As well as the writing, the marlin was on the wall… Lucille and Desi pose for yet another publicity picture.

The State of the Union

The fights started very early in the marriage. Within days of their wedding at the Byram Bridge Club, Connecticut, Lucille vented her fury with Desi by taking a hammer to his brand-new station wagon. "In those early days," she wrote, "our fights were a kind of love-making. Desi and I enjoyed them… Often I phoned DeDe at three a.m. to recite our latest, loudest, and most passionate fight."

Although Lucille always insisted that she was deeply in love with Desi, she found it increasingly difficult to put up with his gambling, drinking, and womanizing. Also, though she claimed that she had known from the beginning that "Latin men expect their wives to take a secondary role", it was not in her nature to play the part of the little woman. There were separations, but they never lasted more than a day or two. "During that first year of our marriage," Desi told a reporter, "every time Lucy and I fought, I packed my clothes and moved to a Hollywood hotel."

In 1944, Lucille filed for divorce on the grounds of mental cruelty. Significantly, she chose to file in California where divorce proceedings took a whole year to process. On the night before she was due to attend court, Lucille changed her mind and there was a "passionate" reconciliation; whether it blew hot or cold, the marriage was always passionate. Lucille recorded that her change of mind cost her $2,000.

Five years later, Lucille and Desi renewed their vows and were married in a Catholic ceremony. "I closed my eyes," wrote Lucille, "put blinders on, and ignored what was too painful to think about… I tried to curb my temper."

It worked, temporarily, and the arrival of their two much-loved children helped enormously. But the writing was on the wall…

Above: (*left to right*) British actress Anna Lee, Lucille, and Clark Gable take a break from rehearsing a CBS Screen Guild program in 1950.

Opposite above: Lucille with comedian and film star Danny Kaye—they were frequent guests on each other's *TV Specials*. Glass in hand, Desi Arnaz (*right*) looks on.

Opposite below: Lucille and Dean Martin at Desi and Lucille's surprise 13th Wedding Anniversary party, December 16, 1953.

A Lucille Ball-type Roll

In 1949 Lucille signed a contract with Harry Cohn at Columbia to make a film a year for four years. In fact, she made six films in two years—three for Columbia, two for Paramount, and one for RKO. But some of the Hollywood magic had evaporated, and Lucille, who was longing to have a baby and was in danger of becoming type-cast, began to look for a way out of the movie business.

The end, when it came, was farcical. While still obligated to make one more film for Cohn, Lucille complained about the quality of the parts she was being offered. Cohn's response was to insist that she play the lead in one of Columbia's notoriously dreadful B movies—an Arabian Nights shocker called *The Magic Carpet*. Cohn expected Lucille to refuse, in which case he would have her at his mercy, but Lucille was made of sterner stuff. Although pregnant, she accepted the part of Princess Narah, made the film in five days, took the $85,000 fee, and left.

Left above: On the TV studio set, Don Grady (*left*) directs a master class in "kissing", with Lucille and John Hodiak as demonstrators, while two young actors look on. Hodiak and Lucille appeared together in the 1948 MGM film *Two Smart People*.

Left below: Lucille and Desi with a musical gag at a City of Hope Benefit Night at the Racquet Club, Palm Springs in 1953.

Opposite: Eartha Kitt, Desi, and Lucille with the thirteenth Wedding Anniversary cake at Larry Finlay's Restaurant, Sunset Strip, Los Angeles, December 16, 1953.

Above: Sammy Davis Jr. as Lieutenant Pinkerton and Lucille as Madame Butterfly take part in a charity benefit show in aid of relief for the victims of Super Typhoon Vera, the worst storm in Japan's history, September 1959.

Opposite: (*left to right*) Desi, Lucille, and Bob Hope in 1955. Lucille, both a friend and a fan of Hope, used to say "You spell Bob Hope C-L-A-S-S".

"We never had a romance. Nothing after hours"
– Bob Hope on his friendship with Lucille

Above: Lucille and Desi pose in front of the long, long trailer that featured in the film of the same name. It was the first film they made together, and was one of the hits of 1954.

Opposite: At the height of their popularity, Lucille and Desi take a winter break with Desi Junior, Lucie, and the family's dog.

Left above and below: Lucille and Desi greet the crowds of fans on their publicity tour to promote *The Long, Long Trailer*. They flew to New York, where the movie had its premiere at Radio City Music Hall.
Right: Lucille and Desi receive a symbolic key to MGM Studios from E. J. "Eddie" Mannix, studio executive, July 1954.

The Long, Long Trailer

Lucille took barely two months off work for the arrival of Desi Junior before returning to work on the third series of *I Love Lucy*. As soon as that was completed, she and Desi reported to the MGM lot to make *The Long, Long Trailer*, partly as a favor to the producer, Lucille's old friend Pandro S. Berman. MGM had doubts about making the film, arguing that fans might not pay to see Lucille and Desi in a film when they could watch them for nothing on television. Never one to miss a chance of gambling, Arnaz placed a bet with the studio that it would make more money than the highest-grossing comedy movie at that time (*Father of the Bride*). The film took in $5 million and Desi won his $25,000 bet.

Opposite and left: In happier times… Lucille (as the Dance Hall gal) and Sheriff Desi in fancy dress at a costume party in aid of Share Inc., a mental health charity. The party was held at Ciro's Restaurant, Los Angeles. Like Lucille and Desi's marriage, Ciro's had not long to run. In 1957 its founder and owner, Herman Hoover, was forced to file for bankruptcy.

Cracking Jokes and Cracking Apart

By the late 1950s, Lucille was professionally on the crest of a tidal wave. She was the most famous television star in the world and had become a showbiz idol of gigantic proportions. Privately, life was not so good, and the gossip magazines were beginning to speculate as to how long her marriage to Desi would last. As early as 1955, *Confidential* ran a lead story with the title "Does Desi Really Love Lucy?", and two years later *Behind the Scene* ran "The Inside Story of How Lucy Stays Married to Desi".

Lucille painfully recorded the terminal decline of her marriage in her autobiography, written in 1966, which was hidden for twenty years until her daughter Lucie discovered the manuscript among her mother's papers after Lucille's death. "I realized we never really liked each other," wrote Lucille, with what seems like chilling detachment. "We had a great attraction going for each other at the beginning but we didn't approve of each other… I was able to accept the situation for many years because it was our secret. But when Desi made it public domain, I knew I couldn't be publicly embarrassed any longer…"

By the spring of 1960, Lucille and Desi were totally estranged. She decided to file for divorce. This time there was to be no last-minute reconciliation. Despite the pain of the process, on March 3, 1960, Lucille filed for divorce on the grounds of "extreme mental cruelty". Later that day they filmed the final scene in the last *TV Special* they made together.

Opposite: Lucille and Desi board the special car provided by the Santa Fe Railroad to promote *Forever, Darling*. The cross-country train made stops at Chicago, Detroit, Cleveland, Pittsburgh, Philadelphia, New York City, and Lucille's hometown of Jamestown, New York State.
Left above: With three-year-old Desi Junior in Lucille's arms, Desi and Lucille wave to their fans.
Left below: The unit on location in Yosemite National Park for outdoor scenes from *Forever, Darling*.

Forever Darling

In 1956, Lucille and Desi made their second and last film together. The entire project was swathed in irony. The film's title was *Forever, Darling,* and it told the story of a couple whose five-year-long marriage was beginning to fall apart. Although the film was distributed by MGM, Desi formed his own company to make it: Zanra Productions ("Arnaz" in reverse). The director was Alexander Hall, Lucille's *beau* from the early 1930s.

The film was refused a Radio City Music Hall premiere on the grounds that it wasn't good enough, and was a critical and box office disaster. Everything they did for television had the Midas Touch, but Lucille and Desi never made the grade as movie makers. And perhaps the greatest irony of all was that the film had a happy ending with the marriage being saved by the couple's Guardian Angel, played by James Mason.

Opposite above: Hollywood gossip columnist Louella Parsons chats with Desi and Lucille at the Golden Globe Awards, Cocoanut Grove, Ambassador Hotel, Los Angeles, February 23, 1956.

Opposite below: Lucille at the TV Emmy Awards, Moulin Rouge nightclub, Hollywood, March 7, 1955.

Above: A pensive Lucille on the set of the *Ed Sullivan Show*, New York City, February 5, 1956.

"My only to-die moments in life have been when I've lost my self-respect" - Lucille when Desi's infidelity became public knowledge

Pictures from the 1959 visit to Europe.
Clockwise from top left: Lucie and Desi Junior sample English canapés, London, June 10; Desi Junior (*left*) and Lucie on board the liner *Liberté*; the family arrives in Paris; Lucille and her children at Fontainebleau; with Lucille's cousin Cleo and Cleo's husband Ken Morgan on the steps of St. Peter's in Rome; at a café near Fontainebleau; Lucille and cousin Cleo in Ischia, Italy; Mrs. Mike Chinego, Cleo, and Lucille on the Chinego estate in Italy.

The Last Hope and the Last Straw

The marriage had already hit the rocks by the time Desi was arrested for drunkenness and Lucille subsequently found him in bed with two hookers. In May 1959, a public appearance in Oklahoma City turned into a publicity nightmare for Lucille and, on the advice of their joint marriage counsellors, she and Desi decided to take a six-week break from work and to visit Europe. Lucille broke her toe on the Atlantic crossing and the two of them argued constantly. The children mistook Desi's drunkenness for illness, and were deeply affected by the bickering of their parents. By the time the family reached Rome, Desi Junior was so upset that he refused to leave the hotel room. Immediately after their return to the United States, they separated. "Maybe it can renew and refresh a relationship," Lucille told a reporter, but she knew the situation was hopeless.

Opposite: Clad in a suitably French beret, Desi takes Lucille's photograph on board the *Liberté* as they sail to Southampton, England, May 1959.

Above: Lucille and Desi visit the house of their old friend Maurice Chevalier (*center*), May 22, 1959. Chevalier commiserated with Lucille, but told her there was only pain in staying with Desi once love had died.

Chapter 3

I Love Lucy

1951-1959

Opposite: A scene from *Be a Pal*, Episode 3 of the first series of *I Love Lucy*, aired on October 22, 1951, by which time some 12 million viewers were tuning in to the new show.
Left: Lucy advertises Vitameatavegamin in of the most famous episodes—*Lucy Does a TV Commercial*, aired on May 5, 1952. In making the commercial, Lucy becomes drunk, for the tonic supposedly contains 23 percent alcohol—in fact, it was apple juice. As in so many scenes from *I Love Lucy*, Lucille drew on what she had learned from other comedians—in this case from Red Skelton.

VITAMEATAVEGAMIN
FOR HEALTH

The Making of Lucy

Lucille and Desi created Desilu in 1948. The aim was to establish their own production company which would enable them to make movies together. It didn't work. Their first two projects—*Blazing Beulah from Butte* and *That Townsend Girl*—never got beyond the idea stage. Perhaps as a result, Lucille made her television debut in February 1959 on *The Chesterfield Supper Club Show*. On Christmas Eve the same year, she and Desi appeared together on *The Ed Wynn Show*. They both saw the potential of the medium. Lucille hesitated before committing herself, as Hollywood studio bosses were threatening to blacklist any stars that switched to the new small screen rival, but the spirit of her old friend and idol Carole Lombard appeared to her in a dream to tell her: "Go ahead, honey. Give it a whirl".

Lucille rejected the idea of adapting *My Favorite Husband* for television. She was insistent that she and Desi would appear together as husband and wife. To that end, they developed what many consider the first television sitcom. It was to be farcical in style, chronicling the madcap adventures of Lucy and Desi Ricardo and their neighbors and landlords Fred and Ethel Mertz.

They assembled their team, keeping the writers from *My Favorite Husband*, and bringing in the veteran Czech director of photography Karl Freund, a man who had impressed Lucille during her time at MGM. Desi was to take charge of the production, and the other two acting principals were to be William Frawley and Vivian Vane.

On September 3, 1951, the first reading of the pilot script took place at the General Service Studios in Los Angeles.

"Speeeeeeeeeed it up a little!"

Above: Three moments from the Kramer's Candy Kitchen sequence in the opening episode of Series 2—*Job Switching*, aired on September 15, 1952. (*left to right*) Amanda Milligan, as Candy Dipper, and Lucy Ricardo get into a mess with chocolate; Ethel Mertz and Lucy battle with the conveyor belt; and the end of the chocolate affair.

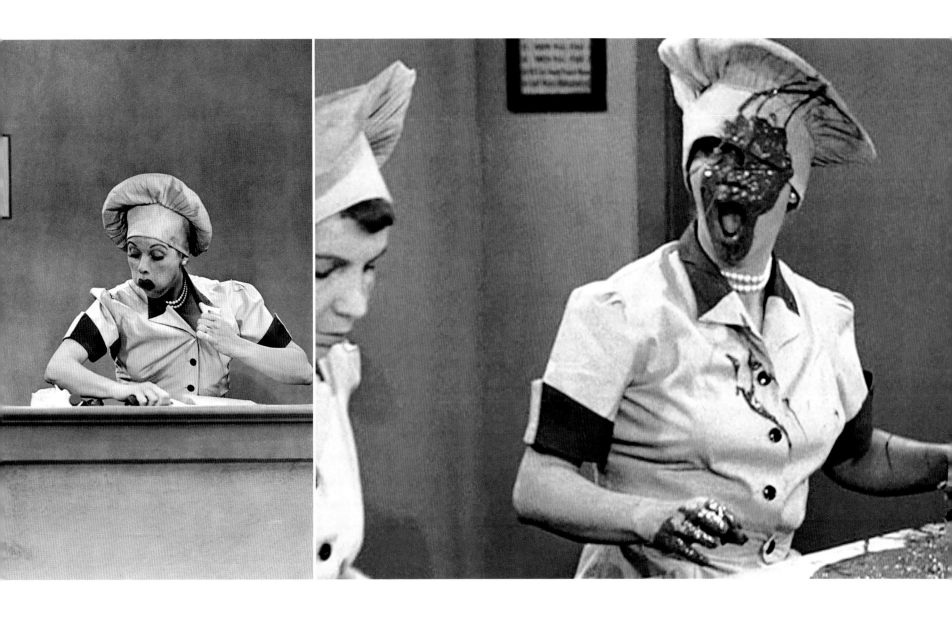

"How *I Love Lucy* was born? We decided that
instead of divorce lawyers profiting from our
mistakes, we'd profit from them" - Lucille

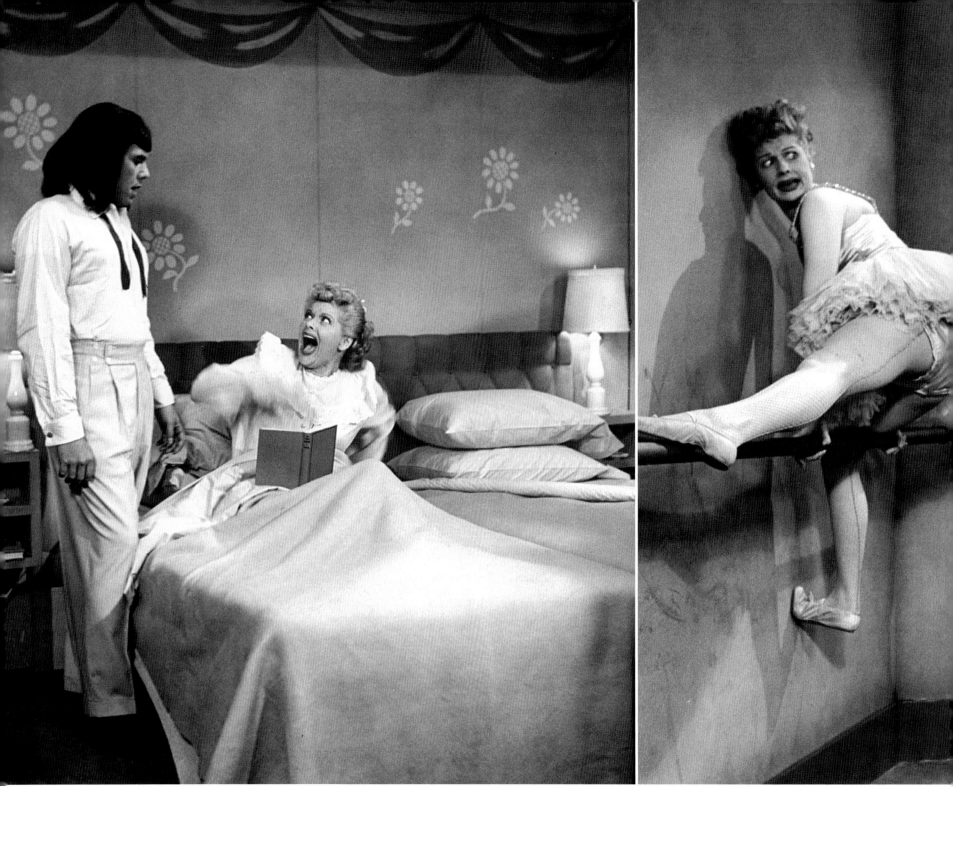

"The hair-stylist (at MGM) changed the style of my hair
from long and loose and flowing to up and lacquered, until I had to
take the crust off it at night by cracking it with a brush" - Lucille

Above left to right: Desi's wig terrifies Lucy in *The Adagio*, Episode 12 of the first series, aired on December 31, 1951; Mary Wicks as the Ballet Teacher gazes in horror as Lucy is trapped on the *barre* in Episode 19, *The Ballet*, aired on February 18, 1952; and an example of classic Lucy comedy *schtick* from episode 6—*The Audition,* aired on November 19, 1951, by which time viewing figures for *I Love Lucy* had risen to 15 million.

Left above and right below:
Two scenes from Episode 23—*The Moustache*, aired on March 17, 1952. Lucy had acquired a beard as retaliation for Desi growing a moustache.
Left below: Lucy bathes her aching feet, from Episode 4, Series 1—*The Diet*, aired on October 29, 1951.
Right above: The shoot-out finale from Episode 21, Series 1—*The New Neighbors*, aired on March 3, 1952.

The First Series

It worked. The tobacco company Philip Morris agreed to sponsor the show (though Lucy had to put the Chesterfield cigarettes that she smoked into a Philip Morris tin when on set), and also agreed that the show should be filmed with a live audience in Los Angeles, but aired from New York. This in itself was a revolution in early television practice, for the cost of filming was considerable. The title was Desi's idea. One day, as he was reading a script he suddenly exclaimed: "I love that Lucy…"

With DeDe in the audience, the first episode (*The Girls Want to Go to a Night Club*) was filmed on September 8, 1951, and aired just over five weeks later, on October 15. Describing that night, Kathleen Brady, Lucille's biographer, has written: "She came on stage as Lucille Ball, but when she made her final bow, she had become forever Lucy Ricardo".

Above and opposite: On the eve of the fourth series of *I Love Lucy*, Ed Sullivan devoted the whole of his CBS peak-time Sunday night show to Lucille and Desi. The show was aired on October 3, 1954, and was then known as *The Talk of the Town*, later to become *The Ed Sullivan Show*. It was a tribute to Lucille and to *I Love Lucy*, which was then approaching its 100th episode, and reached an audience of roughly 50 million viewers.

"She's given the whole world so much darn enjoyment,
Lucille Ball is the best-loved star in show business" –
Ed Sullivan on The Ed Sullivan Show

Ricky: We've got to use our brains.

Lucy: Well, let's see...

Ricky: You stay out of this - on I Love Lucy

Left: The prelude to the grape-wrestling sequence in Episode 23, Series 5—*Lucy's Italian Movie*, aired on April 16, 1956—with Teresa Tirelli as the Wine Stomper. The plot involved Lucy being approached by film director Vittorio Phillipe to appear in his forthcoming movie *Bitter Grapes*—a dig at Silvana Mangano's 1949 film *Bitter Rice*.

Above: The Ricardos and the Mertzes head for Los Angeles in Episode 13 of Series 5—*California, Here We Come!*, aired on January 10, 1955. (*left to right*) Lucille, Vivian Vane, Desi, and William Frawley.

Left: Lucy Ricardo as Superman climbs out on the ledge for Episode 13, Series 6—*Lucy and Superman*, aired on January 14, 1957.

Above: In a program filmed just two months after giving birth to Desi Junior, Lucille as Lucy Ricardo just about copes with Little Ricky Ricardo in Episode 22, Series 2—*No Children Allowed,* aired on April 20, 1953.

The Biggest Audience Yet

When Lucille became pregnant in February 1952, it was Jess Oppenheimer, head-writer on *I Love Lucy,* who suggested that Lucy Ricardo should also have a baby, on television. The CBS censor approved the idea, although the network men in suits ruled out the use of the word "pregnant". In all, seven episodes in succession were allotted to Ricardo pregnancy, from *Lucy is Enceinte* to *Lucy Goes to the Hospital.* The workaholic Lucille continued filming until two months before her baby was due.

The episode in which the baby arrives, watched by 44 million Americans, was aired on the same day as the birth of Lucille and Desi's son, Desi Junior. At the end of the program, over footage of the Ricardo's baby, the announcer delivered a message from the sponsors: "May their lives together be filled with as much joy and laughter and carefree happiness as they have brought all of us week after week. To Lucy, to Ricky, and to the new baby: love and kisses from Philip Morris and from all America".

Opposite above: The studio audience for *I Love Lucy* stand in line outside the Desilu Playhouse. One fan who never missed a show was Lucille's mother DeDe, who had a seat specially reserved for her.

Opposite below: A publicity still of the Mertzes and the Ricardos.

Above left: A scene from Episode 29, Series 2 —*The Camping Trip*, aired on June 8, 1953.

Above right: Lucy and Ethel pose as Women from Mars in Episode 23, Series 3—*Lucy is Envious,* aired on March 29, 1954.

Time out from being Lucy and Ricky…
Above from left to right: Desi and
Lucille at the racetrack (success fuelled
Desi's addiction to gambling); Desi
serenades Lucille on location; Lucille wears
her favorite piece of jewelry, an aquamarine
and ruby ring given to her by Desi, on a
night out at a Los Angeles restaurant.

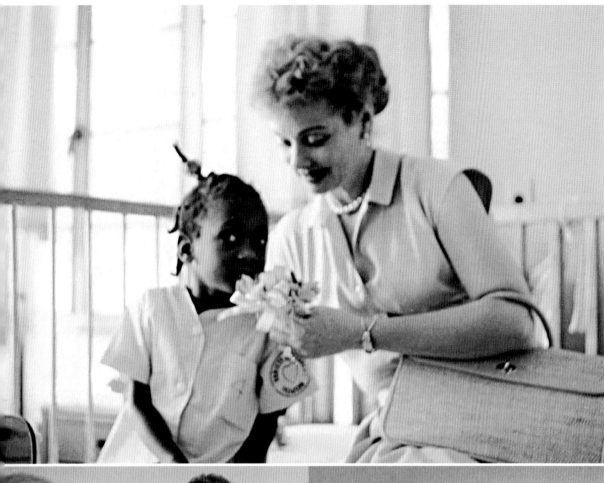

Left: Two photographs covering a visit made by Lucille, Vivian, William, and Desi to a children's hospital in New York, where they visited crippled and bedridden children, and later planted a tree. Lucille kept her charity work in low profile, but did much to help the Barbara David Center for Childhood Diabetes in Denver and the Shiners' Hospital for Crippled Children in Springfield, Massachusetts.

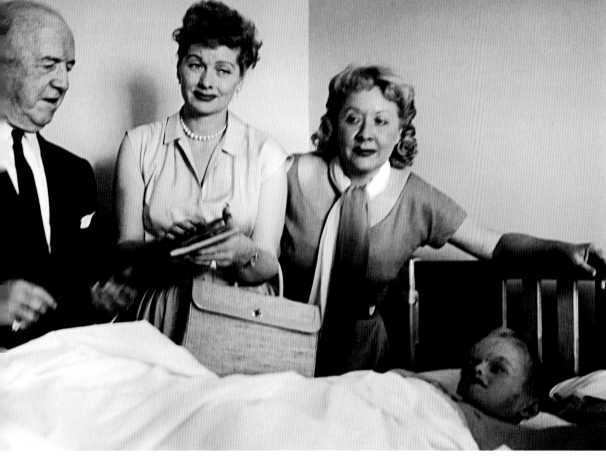

The Heart of Lucille

How pleasant it would have been for Lucille if her real life could have been as zany and carefree as that of Lucy Ricardo. There is always a happy ending in *I Love Lucy*. Come what may, Lucy and Ricky are always reconciled, suspicion is always proved to be groundless, peace is always made, and love always triumphs. It has to be that way. From the very beginning, Lucille and Desi established rules governing the storylines and characterization of Lucy Ricardo: the humor is never to be mean or unkind; Lucy is never to be seen in danger; she should never knowingly get drunk; no show should ever contain "blue" or vulgar material; and Lucy and Ricky must not share a bed. Given such healthy parameters, there was little in Lucy Ricardo's life that could go seriously wrong.

Real life was different. Throughout the five and a half years of *I Love Lucy*, Lucille was constantly anxious about the state of her marriage. For several months in 1952, she was concerned about her pregnancy. And in 1953, she was subjected to a hate campaign run by the House Un-American Activities Committee (HUAC).

HUAC reopened their investigation into Lucille's voter registration way back in 1936, when her grandfather, Fred Hunt, had persuaded her to register as a Communist. Philip Morris fell silent. MGM did nothing to restore Lucille's confidence. The *Los Angeles Herald-Express* ran a three-inch headline "LUCILLE BALL NAMED RED", accompanied by a photograph of her registration card, with the cancellation of her membership of the Communist Party erased.

Desi stood firmly behind her, publicly declaring "the only thing red about that girl is her hair and even that we're not so sure about". In the end Lucille was exonerated by the Committee, and of the 4,000 letters she received from the public, only two were critical.

Above: On behalf of the cast of *I Love Lucy*, Lucille (*center*) and Desi (*right*) receive the key to the city of Miami, Florida, from Mayor Randy Christmas (*left*), at the Dinner Key Auditorium, November 25, 1956.

Opposite: On the same visit to Florida, Lucille congratulates a winning jockey at the Tropical Park racetrack in Miami-Dade County.

"I knew Latins had a mother complex, but I didn't know Desi hated his mother!" – Lucille

Previous pages: Lucille, Desi Junior and the poodles in the garden of their house on Roxbury Drive, Beverly Hills, 1957. Jack Benny lived next door.

Left: Same dogs, same five-bedroom five-bathroom house, same garden—but the dress has been changed, and the drum major has departed.

"I am a real ham. I love an audience. I work better with an audience. I am dead, in fact, without one" – Lucille

The Fruits of Success

On April 4, 1957 the team filmed *The Ricardos Dedicate a Statue*, the last half-hour episode of *I Love Lucy*. In the same month, Lucille and Desi signed a $12-million contract with Westinghouse for a series of one-hour comedy specials, each of which featured guest stars. That there was still plenty of gas in the tank was proved by the enthusiasm with which Lucille and Desi approached the first show. Even when edited, it ran for seventy-five minutes, and it gained *The US Steel Hour* its highest rating ever.

A couple of months later, Lucille and Desi put in a bid to buy RKO Studios from the General Tire and Rubber Company, who were running the studios at a loss. Lucille played no part in the negotiations. She didn't see the need for such an extravagant action, but the fact that the money was there was largely thanks to her. "As I signed away $6,150,000," she wrote, "my hand shook… I never saw much real cash and never really *felt* rich either." It was a far cry from the day in 1932 when she first walked into RKO for a showgirl call after being fired from Columbia Pictures.

Lucille and Desi made thirteen one-hour comedy specials together, the last being *Lucy Meets the Moustache* with guest stars Ernie Kovacs and Edie Adams. It was filmed on March 2, 1960. "In the final scene," Lucille recalled, "Desi was supposed to pull me into an embrace and kiss me. When the scene arrived and the cameras closed in, we just looked at each other, and then Desi kissed me, and we both cried."

The following day, she filed for divorce.

Opposite: Lucy in full toreador outfit for Episode 23, Series 4—*Bull Fight Dance*, aired on March 28, 1955. The dance was part of a fantasy sequence when Lucy imagines how she will appear on Ricky's "Heart Fund" show.

Lucy Ricardo

I Love Lucy was always a team effort, and Lucille was not the only member of the cast to be recognized as outstanding. William Frawley and Vivian Vance, as well as the team of writers (Jess Oppenheimer, Madelyn Pugh Davis, Bob Carroll, and later Bob Schiller and Bob Weiskopf) received Emmy nominations, but the show owed its phenomenal success to Lucille. Her portrayal of the childishly enthusiastic, scatter-brained housewife was the central delight of every episode, whether she was posing as saxophonist, toreador, geisha, sculptress, bellboy, hot-dog vendor or, more specifically, Carmen Miranda, the Maharincess of Franistan, Camille Queen of the Gypsies, or Gary Cooper.

The time she had spent working with Red Skelton, the Marx Brothers, and even the Three Stooges had provided her with an apprenticeship in visual humor, on top of which she had been coached by Buster Keaton, the greatest movie clown of them all. In all the famous set-pieces of clowning that she performs (among them the baking of the eighteen-foot loaf, setting fire to her own (artificial) nose, and the fake mirror act with Harpo Marx), Lucille extracts the optimum amount of humor, while maintaining a true Keaton sobriety.

She saved the best almost for last. On February 7, 1957, the audience gathered at Desilu Studios for Episode 20, Series 6—*Lucy Does the Tango*. The storyline centered on the Ricardos and the Mertzes setting up an egg farm. Commercially, it's a disaster, so Lucy and Ethel smuggle in shop-bought eggs. To hide what they are doing, Lucy stuffs eggs down her blouse. Ricky insists they practice their tango for a PTA benefit. The eggs crack, and run down inside Lucy's clothing. Her wonderfully crafted reaction produced a studio laugh that lasted for over a minute.

Opposite: Lucille, as Lucy Ricardo in dance girl costume, with one of her millions of adoring fans.
Left: Lucille and Desi attend a charity ball in the 1950s. Both were fond of wearing Western outfits and lived a ranch-house lifestyle for much of their married life.

Lucy's Empire Expands

Professionally, the *I Love Lucy* years were the happiest and the most successful in Lucille's life. She loved performing and basked in the security of being the star of an enormously popular show. While Desi ran the business, Lucille adopted the role of Mom, choosing the curtains for the set, checking each "pillow, picture, pot, and pan that went into the Ricardos' apartment to make sure it was authentically middle income", and even cleaning the bathroom and kitchen. She was bossy, in a motherly way, friendly to all, but seldom expressing her appreciation of the work done by writers and technicians. She left all that

to Desi, whose business acumen and technical expertise she greatly admired. While Desi kept his drink dependence under control, all went well.

The studio became a second home to Lucille and Desi. They adapted the existing accommodation from the old RKO days to provide them with a suite that consisted of two large dressing rooms, a bathroom, living room, and a dining room. There was also a kitchen in which, on many nights after the show, Desi or Willie Mae Barker (housekeeper and later nanny to their children) cooked a dinner for fifty or sixty guests.

By 1957, Desilu owned and produced

several other top TV shows, among them *The Wyatt Earp Show*, *The Eve Arden Show*, and *Make Room for Daddy* (starring comedian Danny Thomas). Five years later, Lucille bought Desi's controlling interest in the company, to become the first woman president of a major TV studio. Under her presidency, Desilu went from strength to strength, with Lucille backing such successes as *The Untouchables*, *Mission: Impossible*, and *Star Trek*. Lucille referred to *Star Trek* as "the USO show". "She mistook UFO for USO," explained Herbert Sodow, Head of Production at Desilu. "What else would stars have been to her?"

Left: Desi and Lucille in front of their trophy cabinet, February 1953. The three Awards were for Best Situation Comedy 1952, Best Comedian or Comedienne (Lucille) 1952, and Most Outstanding Personality (Lucille) 1953.

Above: Lucille and Desi arrive at a CBS party in honor of Johnny Carson, June 30, 1955. It was the first season of *The Johnny Carson Show*.

Above: Columnist Hedda Hopper and Lucille at a party celebrating the opening of Canadian-born singer Giselle McKenzie's own TV show, August 28, 1957. Lucille recorded with pride: "Hedda Hopper says that I am one of the few actresses in Hollywood who survived success in a single piece"

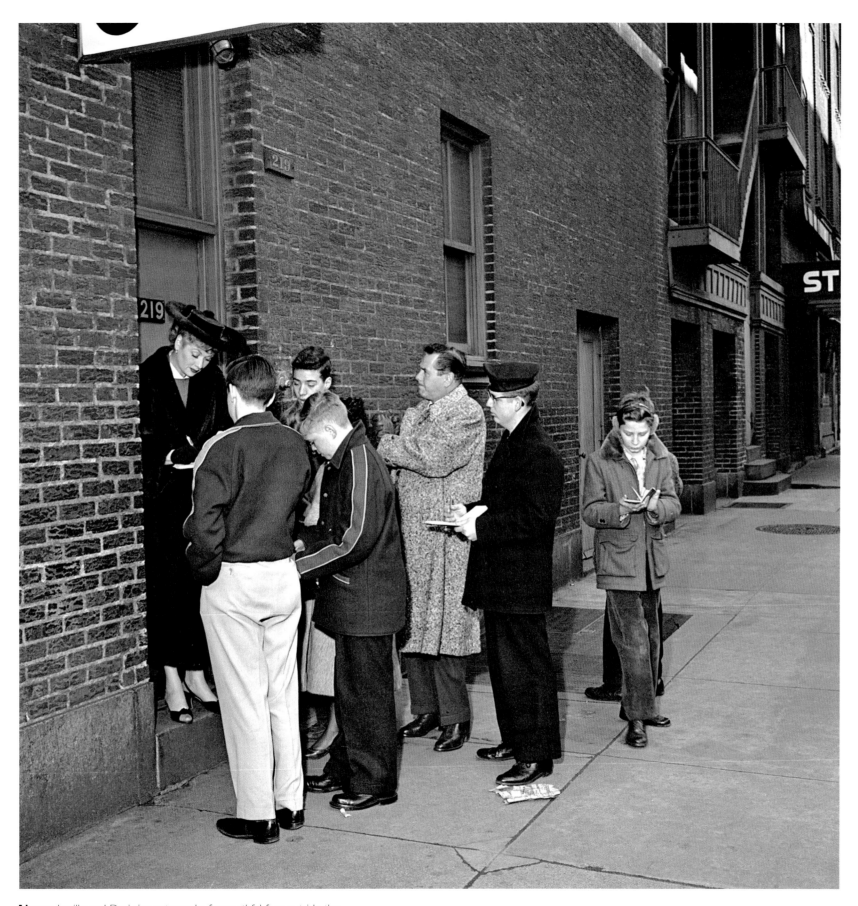

Above: Lucille and Desi sign autographs for youthful fans outside the CBS-TV Studio 50 theater, New York City, February 5, 1956. They were there as guests on the *Ed Sullivan Show*.

Left and right: Two photographs taken at the Desilu employees' summer picnic in the 1950s—in the right-hand picture, Lucille is in the center, wearing the headscarf that was almost part of her "Mom's" uniform. The picnic was an annual affair that Lucille may well have enjoyed more than anyone.

One Big Happy Family

With her own mother DeDe by her side much of the time, Lucille's sense of mothering was constantly to the fore. Desilu and *I Love Lucy* were more than just the major players in her career; they were also her children. In her own words: "It was tremendously exciting building a new company; from seven employees we had grown to one thousand, and not one of them had resigned in Desilu's five years of existence. It was a young organization—our employee's average age was thirty-two—and a sense of family was always emphasized, between company picnics, bowling contests, trips to Disneyland, and New Year's Eve parties at the ranch, where Desi presided like a grand *patrón*."

Lucille was forty years old when *I Love Lucy* began its six-year run, and the old cliché that "Life begins at Forty" proved to be true. She loved the youthfulness of what she was doing. Television was still a young medium, and she and Desi did much to shape its future. Both technically and artistically they were true pioneers.

When the show's run came to an end, Lucille found herself with time and energy on her hands. As a young actress in the 1930s, she had benefited from a theater workshop established at RKO by Lela Rogers (mother of Ginger Rogers). In 1958, Lucille decided to revive such a scheme, on the same lot and in the same theater, which needed a $90,000 renovation. Her accountants referred to it as "Lucy's Folly". Lucille selected sixteen youngsters, all "talented, eager, and tireless"—chips off the old block. To her delight, more than half of them landed television or movie contracts. Running the workshop and rehearsing ten or twelve hours a day on *The Lucy Show* took her mind off domestic troubles.

Above: Queen of All She Surveys… Desi and Lucille take a rooftop view of the Desilu Studios, part of their vast TV realm, August 1959.

Chapter 4

"The Only Way is Up..."

1961-1971

Previous pages: (*left to right*) Gary
Morton, Lucie, Lucille, and Desi Junior.
Opposite: Lucille as Wildcat Jackson and
Keith Andes as Joe Dynamite in the
Broadway production of *Wildcat*, Alvin
Theater, New York City, December 16, 1960.
Left: Lucille and Frank Sinatra at a Western
Motif fundraising party sponsored by SHARE,
Moulin Rouge, New York City, May 14, 1960.

Wildcat

The woman formerly known as Lucille
Ball virtually disappeared from public
cognizance halfway through the first
series of *I Love Lucy*. She was replaced by
her television look-alike, Lucy Ricardo.
On the street she was hailed as "Lucy".
People called out "Lucy, we love you!",
"Good luck, Lucy!", and "We're with you,
Lucy." They told her how she should
handle her husband "Ricky", how she
should deal with Fred Mertz, and how
lucky she was to have a friend like Ethel.

The real Lucille, however, was live and
well, and eager to face new professional
challenges. In September 1960, with
DeDe and the children, she moved to
New York where she had been offered
the lead in the Broadway musical
Wildcat. The venture posed problems.
Lucille was neither a trained singer nor
dancer; she was nearing fifty, and she had
suffered a serious leg injury while filming
The Facts of Life with Bob Hope. But she
flung herself into the show with all her
old energy. The critics were bored, the
audiences were enraptured—the
trouble was they loved the show, not
because of Lucille's performance, but
because of "Lucy's".

Left: Lucille and Gary Morton, a picture taken not long after they first met in Danny's Hideaway, New York, in December 1961. At the time, Morton claimed that he had never seen *I Love Lucy*.

Right: Ever faithful to her Chesterfields, Lucille takes a break on the set of the TV special *The Good Years*, in which she co-starred with Henry Fonda, Mort Sahl, and Margaret Hamilton, November 1961.

"Desi was the great love of my life, I will miss him until the day I die. But I don't regret divorcing him. I just couldn't take it any more"
– Lucille

Previous page, left: Lucille hits the timbers with Jerry Lewis on the opening night of his Los Angeles restaurant, February 1962.
Previous page, right: Lucille with Gary Morton at their table that same night.

Three bits of business from *The Lucy Show* of 1962 and *Here's Lucy* in 1969.
Left above: Lucille, disguised as Chaplin's Little Fellow, hooks comedian Dick Martin in the New Year edition, 1962.
Left below: Lucille keeps the doctors at bay in *Here's Lucy*.
Right: Lucille and Vivian Vance in *Lucy and her Electric Mattress*, November 8, 1962.

"It's hard to make me laugh. I observe, I smile, but when I'm really amused you can hear me a block away" – Lucille

Above left: Lucille as Lucille
Carmichael in an episode of *The Lucy
Show* entitled *Lucy the Music Lover*,
aired on November 19, 1962.
Center: A promotional portrait of
the cast of *The Lucy Show*: (*left to right*)
Jimmy Gerrett (*in front*), Candy Moore,
Lucille, Vivian Vance, and Ralph Hart,
August 24, 1962.
Right: Vivian Vance (as Vivian Bagley)
and Lucille (as Lucille Carmichael) in
Lucy Becomes an Astronaut, aired on
November 5, 1962.

Vivian: How do you like the new skating rink? I hear it's beautiful.

Lucille: I wouldn't know. All I saw was the ceiling.

- from *Lucy the Good Skate*

Keeping it in the family…
Left: Desi Junior (*right*) makes his debut appearance in the first series of *The Lucy Show* with his sister Lucie (*center*) and Lucille. At this time, Desi Senior was still head of Desilu and producer of the show.
Right: Desi Junior watches the show from his seat beneath the bleachers originally built for *I Love Lucy*.

"You see much more of your children once they leave home" – Lucille

Opposite and left: Two studies of Lucille in her New York Hilton Hotel apartment in 1965. She was a top media executive and regarded by many as The Most Famous Woman in the World, but the fashion-model poise and elegance that she had acquired in the early 1930s never left her.

New Husband, New Horizons

Lucille came away from the 171-performance run of *Wildcat* on Broadway with two possessions that lasted for the rest of her life: her theme song and hit of the show, *Hey, Look Me Over,* and a new partner.

It was her fellow actress Paula Stewart who engineered the first meeting of Lucille and stand-up comedian Gary Morton, one week after the opening of *Wildcat.* Paula persuaded Lucille to come to their favorite pizza joint in New York to "meet a great guy". In Lucille's version of the meeting, she told Morton to light her cigarette and he refused. In other versions, Morton leant forward to shake her hand, thereby dipping the end of his tie in her coffee. He put pepper on the tie. Lucille called him a fool and put salt on it. "When that first evening ended," she wrote, "I felt more like myself than I had in months… I guess it didn't take Gary long to realize that beneath my rather brassy exterior, I'm very soft and dependent."

Lucille had fallen for the big, tanned six-footer with the broad shoulders. She needed someone strong, on whom she could lean physically and metaphorically. Doctors were pumping her full of antibiotics, and she was gulping oxygen backstage to keep her going. When she collapsed in mid-performance for the third time during a song-and-dance number, she realized it was time to bring down the curtain.

She flew to London and on to Capri and Rome, "determined", in her words, "to die in a scenic atmosphere". She didn't die but recovery was slow. She returned to the United States, quitting her luxury New York apartment and hurrying back to Beverly Hills. Gary followed her.

Above: Lucille never allowed the extravagance of the setting to overwhelm her sense of the absurd. In Lucille's New York Hilton apartment, she and Gary Morton use wineglasses to clown for the camera.

Right: A bed fit for a queen... Lucille sips her breakfast coffee on a sunny morning in the mid-1960s.

"Behind every successful actress are a hairdresser and a mother" – Lucille

Left: Anthony Newley (as Anthony Fitz-Faversham) takes Lucille (as Lucille Carmichael) for a sidecar view of the Swinging City during the filming of the *Lucy in London Special* for *The Lucy Show*, May 31, 1966. Among others in the cast were The Dave Clark Five, Wilfrid Hyde-White, Robert Morley, and Peter Wyngarde.

Left: Lucille cuts a ribbon of 70mm film to mark the merger of two Hollywood studios, Paramount and Desilu, July 1967. With her is Charles G. Bluhdorn, Board Chairman of Gulf & Western. The deal cost Gulf & Western $17 million, of which $10 million went to Lucille. She insisted that no former employees of Desilu should lose their jobs.

Make Someone Happy

When she returned from New York to Beverly Hills, Lucille invited Gary Morton to stay in her guesthouse while she convalesced. He repeatedly brought up the subject of marriage, but it wasn't until DeDe told her that she "shouldn't let that guy get away" that Lucille succumbed. Gary proposed while they were both flying back to New York—Lucille to do a TV show with Henry Fonda, and Gary to appear at the Copacabana. She hedged for a moment, for there had been none of the instant mutual passion that had sparked between her and Desi twenty years earlier. But she agreed to marry Gary. "From that moment, I had no qualms, no apprehension. We liked each other before we loved each other." A few days later, they were married by Dr. Norman Vincent Peale at his Marble Collegiate Church in Manhattan on November 19, 1961. The organ played their theme song—*Make Someone Happy*.

Unlike Desi, Gary was not a high flyer. Nor was he addicted to drinking or gambling, although he did show an obsessive liking for golf. Had she wished to, Lucille could have settled down to spend the rest of her life in ease and comfort. The children were growing up. They accepted Gary without fuss. DeDe was in good health and the relationship between mother and daughter remained close. Lucille and Gary had fun enlarging and re-designing the house on Roxbury Drive. Lack of money was unlikely ever to be a problem.

But the old drive to succeed and the new addiction to mass popularity made retirement unthinkable.

Previous page, left: Lucille relaxes at home. She was proud of the fabrics and furnishings, which were always her choice.

Previous page, right: Lucille the artist… one of her favorite painters was Grandma Moses.

Opposite: Lucille and Henry Fonda on location for a scene from the 1968 movie *Yours, Mine, Ours*. The film was a considerable commercial success. Years later, Jane Fonda reported that her father had been "deeply in love" with Lucille at the time.

Above: Gary Morton (*extreme left*) and Lucille at the Emmy Awards Party, May 19, 1968. Lucille had just been presented with the Award for Outstanding Continued Performance by an Actress in a Leading Role in a Comedy series.

Opposite: Lucille arrives for the Lucy Day festivities at the New York World's Fair. August 31, 1964. "The World's Most Beloved Redhead" was being feted as "a truly significant force for international goodwill and understanding". Lucille left her handprints on the sidewalk at the Fair's site, next to those of her friend Hedda Hopper.

"The secret of staying young is to live honestly, eat slowly, and lie about your age" – Lucille

The Lucy Show

Now in her fifties, Lucille maintained a prodigious workload throughout the 1960s. Besides starring in 156 episodes of *The Lucy Show* for CBS TV, she made four movies: *The Facts of Life* (1961) and *Critics Choice* (1963), both with Bob Hope; *A Guide for the Married Man* (1967) with Walter Matthau; and *Yours, Mine, Ours* (1968) with Henry Fonda. Lucille enjoyed all four films, especially those she made with Bob Hope. They were old friends, and when Hope quipped that he didn't want *The Facts of Life* to become *Road to Infidelity*—a reference to the many *Road* films that he had made with Bing Crosby—Lucille responded by saying: "Bob and I always see eye to eye, especially at the keyhole of my dressing room".

The Lucy Show was originally entitled *The Lucille Ball Show*, but CBS and Desilu gave way to public perception of Lucille as forever being "Lucy". For the first season, the show's four executive producers were Elliott Lewis, Lucille, Gary Morton, and Desi Arnaz. There was friction between Gary and Desi, the latter seeing Gary as the man who had usurped him in the eyes of his former wife and their children. Increasingly, Desi arrived at the studio much the worse for drink, and by the end of the series he agreed to let Lucille buy him out.

Lucille won individual Emmys in 1968 and 1969, and the show featured in the Nielsen Ratings Top Ten every season that it ran. It also attracted celebrity guest stars, among them Jack Benny, Richard Burton and Elizabeth Taylor, George Burns, John Wayne, and Dean Martin. The one disaster was *Lucy and the Lost Star*, with guest Joan Crawford. Lucille discovered Crawford sipping 100 percent proof vodka through a straw on set. The two had a blazing row that left Crawford sobbing on the studio floor.

Opposite: (*left to right*) Desi Junior, Gary, Lucille, and Lucie in Western casual style at a charity fund-raising event.

Above: Gary and Lucille at home in Beverly Hills in the 1960s. The wallpaper and the pictures were Lucille's choice. The TV console may well have been a joint decision.

Left: Gary and Lucille at a party for the Emmy Award nominees held at the Beverly Hills Hotel in May 1967.

Above: (*left to right*) Lucie Arnaz, Lucille, and Gary at a party to
raise money for the SHARE charity, May 19, 1969. At the time,
relations between Lucie and Lucille were strained by Lucie's
decision to marry Phil Vandervort.
Left: Lucille and DeDe at another SHARE charity event in 1970.

Left: The Chesterfield Girl lives and breathes in the London Hilton, February 21, 1968. Her visit to England arose out of *The Lucy Show* episode *Lucy Flies to London*. As a follow-up, CBS wanted a one-hour special set in London. It has not aged well.

"The only way I can play a funny scene is to believe it. Then I can convincingly eat like a dog under a table, freeze to death beneath burning-hot klieg lights, or bake a loaf of bread ten-feet long" –
Lucille

Chapter 5

Golden Girl

1971-1989

Previous page: Lucille attends the Eisenhower Memorial Hospital Benefit Ball, New York City, April 18, 1971. The Benefit was hosted by Lucille's long-time friend, Bob Hope.

Left: Lucie Arnaz marries Phil Vandervort, July 17, 1971. (*left to right*) Lucille, the groom, the bride, and Desi Arnaz.

Above: (*left to right*) Desi Junior, Lucille, and Gary Morton at the annual Thalian Ball, October 1970. The guest being honored was Ed Sullivan.

Above: (*left to right*) Lucille, Vincente Minnelli, Liza Minnelli, Desi Junior, and Vincente Minnelli's fiancée Lee Anderson at the New York premiere of *Cabaret*, February 13, 1972.

Opposite: (*left to right*) Lucille, Liza Minnelli, and Lucie Arnaz turn out to root for Desi Junior as he plays for The Celebrities against the Beverly Hills Police in a fund-raising basketball game for the American Cancer Fund, February 1973.

"She's a great trooper, Liza. I wish I had her talent. If anybody's going to take over from me, it's her"
– Lucille

A time out of war… **Opposite:** Lucille and Desi Arnaz reunite to celebrate Lucie's opening night at the Ahmonson Theater, Los Angeles, in a production of the musical *Seesaw*, September 4, 1974. It was a happy night. The champagne flowed and the show received good notices.

Family Frictions

Lucille once attributed her success in life to "getting rid of what was wrong and replacing it with what is right". Although she had viewed the break-up with Desi as the Number One failure in her life, this philosophy had worked when she divorced Desi and married Gary Morton. It had worked when she quit the big screen and moved to television. But it was not a philosophy that she could apply to life with her own children.

When *Here's Lucy* began its six-year run in 1968, Lucie was seventeen, Desi Junior was fifteen. Both were placed under contract to appear on the show. Although she believed that Desi Junior was the more talented of the two, Lucille carefully counted their lines on each week's script to make sure that they were treated equally. Sadly, however, working with them failed to improve deteriorating parent-child relations. Tiffs that began at home the night before were regularly brought to the studio the following morning, to be re-enacted but not resolved.

Lucie was the first to leave. In July 1969, aged eighteen, she moved into her own apartment, and one year later married her old high school *beau*, Phil Vandervort—a young man of whom Lucille disapproved. Less than a year after the departure of his sister, Desi Junior presented Lucille with greater problems—drink, drugs, and women. He had a penchant for the slightly older woman, and his affair with actress Patty Duke hit all the Hollywood headlines. Lucille hurled threats here, there, and everywhere, including that of charging the actress with statutory rape. Desi Junior left the show.

Ladies of the chorus… **Left:** (*left to right*)
Lucille, Shirley MacLaine, and Ginger Rogers
at Hotel MGM, Las Vegas, on the opening
night of MacLaine's new show *If They Could
See Me Now*, July 1974. MacLaine and
Lucille were not the best of friends. When
they appeared together on a TV show in
1976, the Musical Director Cy Coleman
had to keep them apart so that they
wouldn't fight.

Maimed and Mame

Lucille now had to endure the slings and arrows of bad publicity, as most of the press held her responsible for the break-up of her family. She experienced it as the most wounding time in her life, worse than the persecution she had suffered at the hands of the House Un-American Activities Committee back in 1953. The new generation of gossip magazines clearly did not love "Lucy", and made the most of the birth of Patty Duke's baby in February 1971, despite it being subsequently proved that Desi Junior was not the father.

There were rumors that Lucille was drinking heavily, that she had been banned from a national airline, that she had adopted high-handed and snobbish attitudes. To escape from all this, Lucille fled to her hideaway at the ski-resort of Snowmass, Colorado, where she could live a more-or-less normal life.

Her peace and calm here were brought to an agonizing end in January 1972 when a skier sliced into her, fracturing her right leg and thigh in four places. Lucille was hurried down the mountain on a toboggan, without painkillers, as she had eaten just before the accident occurred. She was taken to hospital where she was anaesthetized and encased in a plaster cast up to her waist. When she recovered consciousness, Lucille was terrified, and removed most of the cast before doctors could stop her.

Weeks later she returned to work, spending almost an entire season of *Here's Lucy* in a wheelchair, and fretting that she would never recover her spirit, her confidence, and her mobility. And yet, a year after the accident, Lucille was back on a film set, dancing and strutting her way through the lead role in the Warner/ABC musical *Mame*.

Left: Lucille strikes a pose for columnist Earl Wilson at a party to celebrate a celebrity showing of *Mame*, given in the Sutton Place town house of investment banker Richard Jennett, February 1974.

Above left: Lucille and DeDe at the SHARE fund-raising party for The Exceptional Children's Foundation for the Mentally Retarded, May 1974.

Above right: Lucille guest stars as Ringmaster in an episode of Desilu's *The Greatest Show on Earth*.

"Mame stayed up all night and drank champagne! What did you expect her to sound like? Julie Andrews?" – Lucille, defending her singing in the movie Mame

Left: With Clint Eastwood by her side, poodle on lap, and Gary Morton sitting behind her, Lucille attends the La Costa Tennis Tournament at the Carlsbad Resort, San Diego, California.

"Fresh out of Clover..."

Desi advised Lucille to stay away from *Mame*, but she went ahead. On the film's release, it was panned by the critics. Pauline Kael described it as "so terrible it isn't boring… We in the audience are not thinking of fun, we're thinking of age and self-deception". According to the *New York Times*: "It's all relentlessly good-natured but unless you've been packed in storage somewhere, it's so familiar that it puts a tremendous burden on its star". Lucille escaped the worst of the criticism, but her wigs came in for adverse comment, as did the amount of Vaseline put on the camera lenses to mask her advancing years.

Perhaps the best thing to come from making the film was the amazing recovery of Lucille's mobility following her accident. Although she accused the choreographer, Onna White, of trying to kill her, by the time shooting finished Lucille could once more kick her foot to eye level in true chorus style.

Worse was to follow. To DeDe's fury, CBS pulled the plug on *Here's Lucy* just after *Mame* opened. For the first time in over twenty years, Lucille was no longer playing the lead in a weekly TV comedy series. There were still plenty of viewers and millions of adoring fans, but network surveys showed that Lucille was not pulling in the younger viewers. She sought revenge on CBS by starring in a TV special called *Lucy Moves to NBC*.

Lucille was not one to go quietly. She was still regularly sent scripts, and she entrusted the task of reading and vetting them to Gary, who turned down *Driving Miss Daisy* on her behalf. But the writing was on the wall. There were always guest spots, but the hosts that invited her on to their shows were also an ageing population.

Left above: Lucille and Flip Wilson at an awards ceremony in the 1970s. In many ways, *The Flip Wilson Show* followed in the footsteps of *I Love Lucy*, gaining the same prestige and winning almost as many awards.
Left below: Another awards ceremony, another outfit.
Right above: Lucille with Jack Lemmon at the Friar's Club Benefit for Milton Berle, Beverly Hills Hilton, October 1973.
Right below: Lucille with Gary and Sammy Davis Jr. at the same Benefit.

Left: The hair is still red, the ring is still on the finger, and there's still a poodle on her lap… Lucille Ball enjoys a day in the sun, 1977.

Right: … and there's still a Chesterfield to hand. Lucille loved to play backgammon, and paid for professional coaching in the game. Every Monday night she took part in backgammon tournaments at a club run by Hugh Hefner.

"My God, I'm outliving my henna!"
– Lucille

Previous spread, left above: Lucille with long-time friend and showbiz colleague, George Burns.

Previous spread, left below: (*left to right*) Frank Sinatra, Lucille, and Gary Morton at the Frank Sinatra Gala "His Friends and His Food", a Benefit for the Desert Hospital held at the Canyon County Club and Hotel, Palm Springs, February 15, 1980.

Previous spread, right: Lucille receives her Cecil B. DeMille Award from Gregory Peck at the 36th Golden Globe Awards, January 27, 1979.

Left: Lucille as Florabelle in *Stone Pillow*.

"Down and out..."

Time took family and friends away. Lucille's faithful maid, Harriet McCain, who had been with Lucille for thirty-five years, died of cancer in the early 1970s. She had accompanied Lucille on her rise to fame, sharing many traumas along the way. Lucille's mother DeDe had said that she hoped Lucille would die before her, "because she can't live without me". It was not to be. DeDe died on July 22, 1977. When Vivian Vance—better known perhaps as Ethel Mertz—died two years later, Lucille was plunged into sorrow. She attempted to lift herself by embarking on an orgy of scrubbing and cleaning at home; "that was her emotional release," said her friend, Marcella Rabwin. "She didn't scream, she got out and cleaned drawers".

Somewhat reluctantly, and against Desi's advice, Lucille agreed to make a TV movie in 1985. It was called *Stone Pillow,* and told the story of Florabelle, an elderly homeless woman, living on the streets of Manhattan. When it was aired, it made the Top Ten list of shows that week, but Lucille decided drama was not for her. She made one last attempt at TV comedy with *Life with Lucy,* teaming up once more with Gale Gordon and hiring her writers from the first days of *I Love Lucy,* Madelyn Pugh Davis and Bob Carroll Junior. Fourteen episodes were written, but only eight were aired before ABC cancelled the show. Lucille was devastated. Two weeks later, Desi died.

There were no more interviews, no more guest spots, but there was one more triumphant public appearance. When Lucille stepped on to the stage, with Bob Hope as her co-presenter, at the 1989 Academy Awards ceremony, she was given a standing ovation. One month later, she died, on April 26, 1989.

Above: (*left to right*) Lucille, Red Buttons, and Vivian Blane at the Friars Tribute to Red Buttons, Waldorf Astoria Hotel, New York City, May 1987.
Opposite: Lucille and Gary Morton arrive at the 6th Annual American Cinema Awards, January 6, 1989.

"For ten minutes you're such a great celebrity. Ten minutes later, you're just another actress" – Lucille

Picture Credits

All images in this book are courtesy of Getty Images, we would also like to thank Jonathan Hyams at Michael Ochs Archive and Mitch Blank for their help. The following images have further attributions:

CBS Photo Archive: 53, 73, 80, 81, 82, 83, 90, 91, 92, 113, 127, 128, 129, 172
Murray Garrett: 35
George Eastman House/Victor Keppler: 28
John Kobal Foundation: 8, 30
Gene Lester: 20, 102, 103, 104
Metronome: 29t
Michael Ochs Archive/ 38, 43, 72b, 88, 89, 130, 152, 163, 166b, 167, 169, 170;
Earl Leaf: 69, 109, 111, 112, 146
Richard Nairin: 168
NBC Television: 142
Popperfoto: 6, 7, 24, 74tl
Silver Screen Collection: 19
Time & Life Pictures: 26, 27, 29b, 49, 52br, 62, 84, 85, 114, 116-117, 122, 123, 126t, 131
Weegee/International Center of Photography: 78
WireImage: 170b, 171, 175